# Where is

by Wendy Body

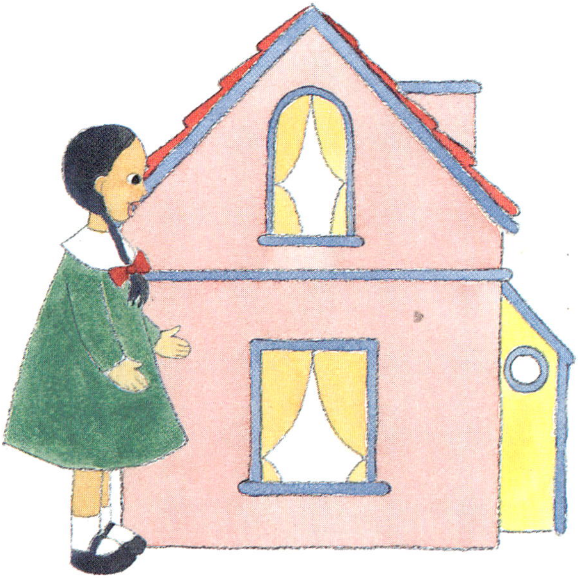

Illustrated by Adrienne Geoghegan

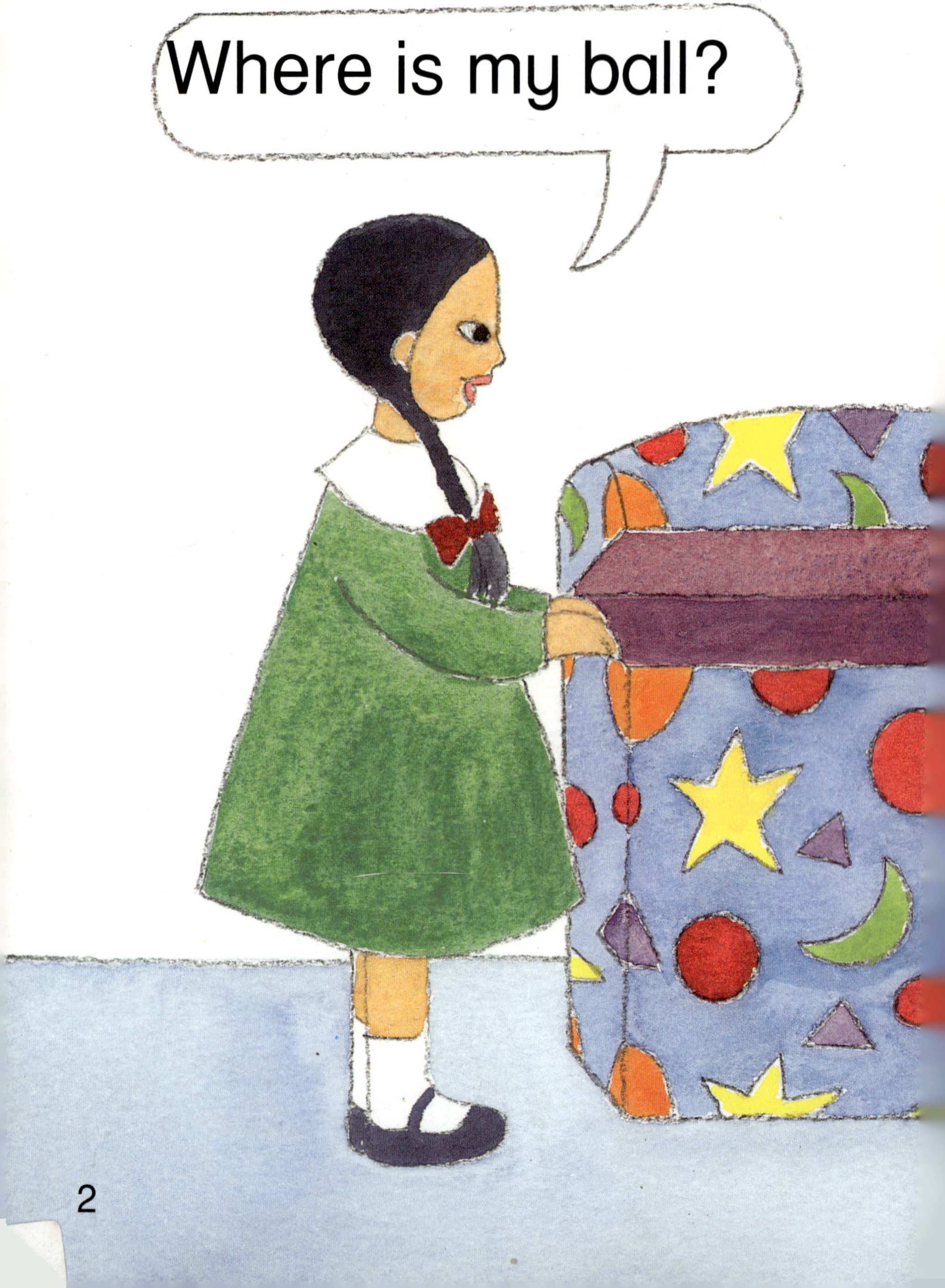
Where is my ball?

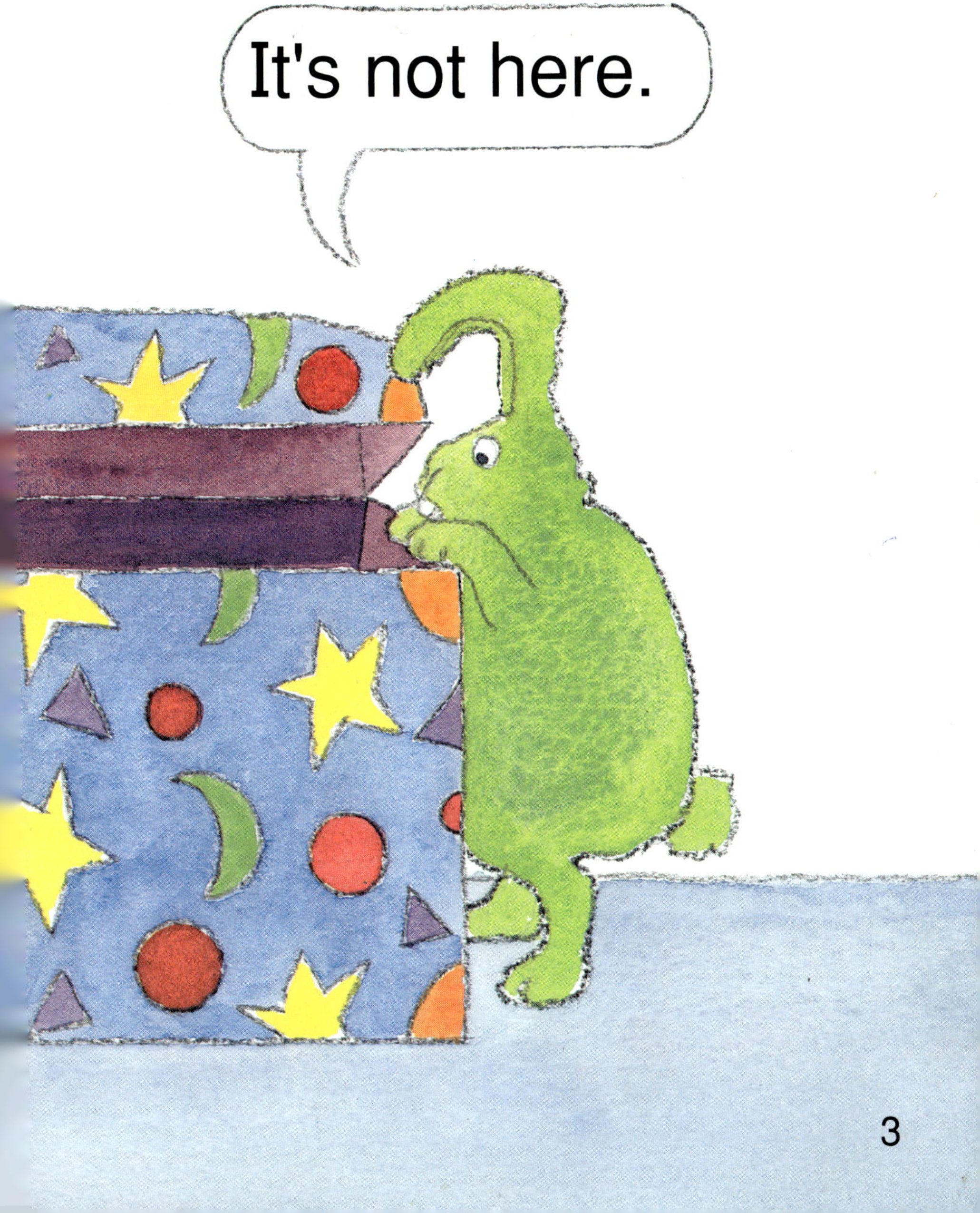
It's not here.

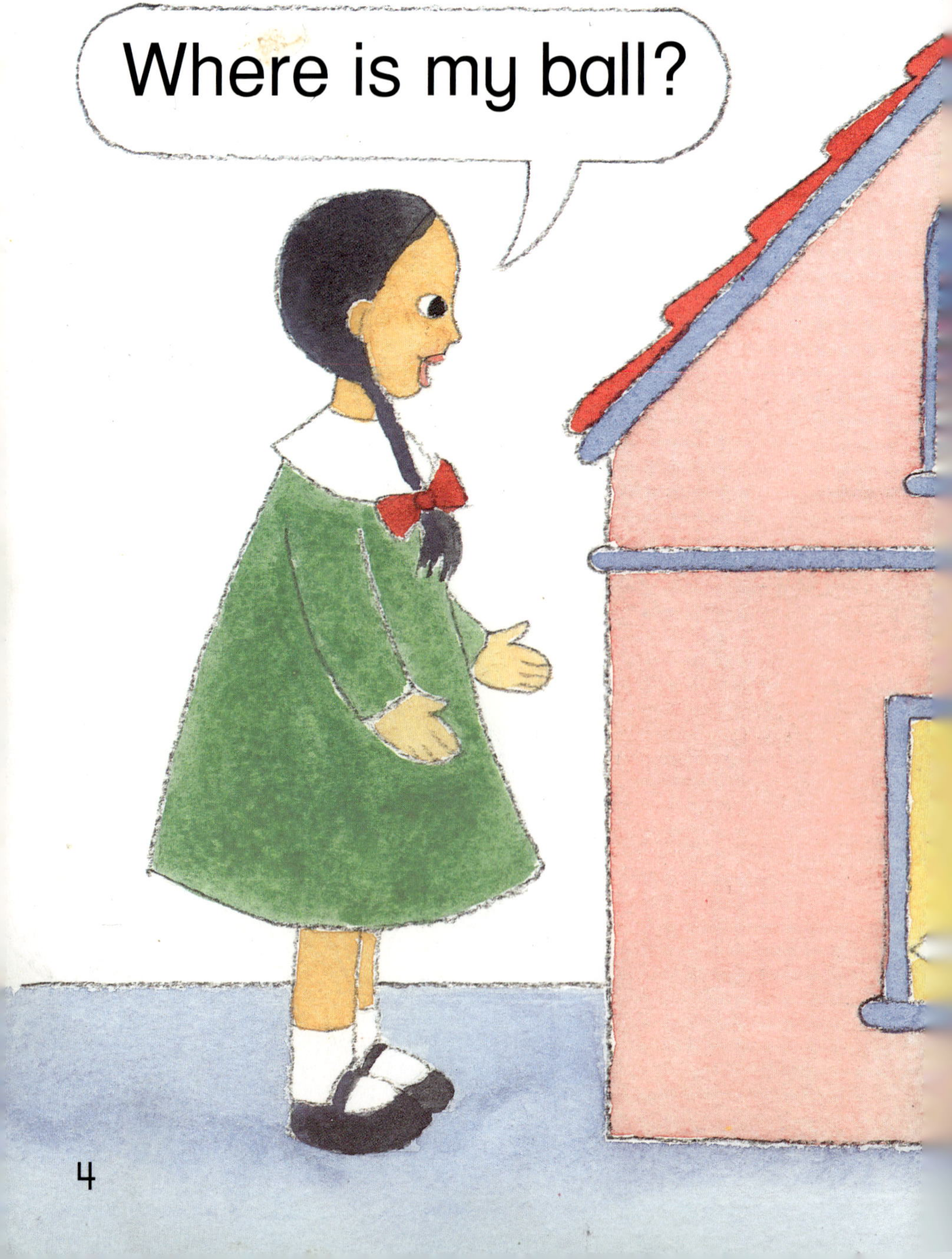
Where is my ball?

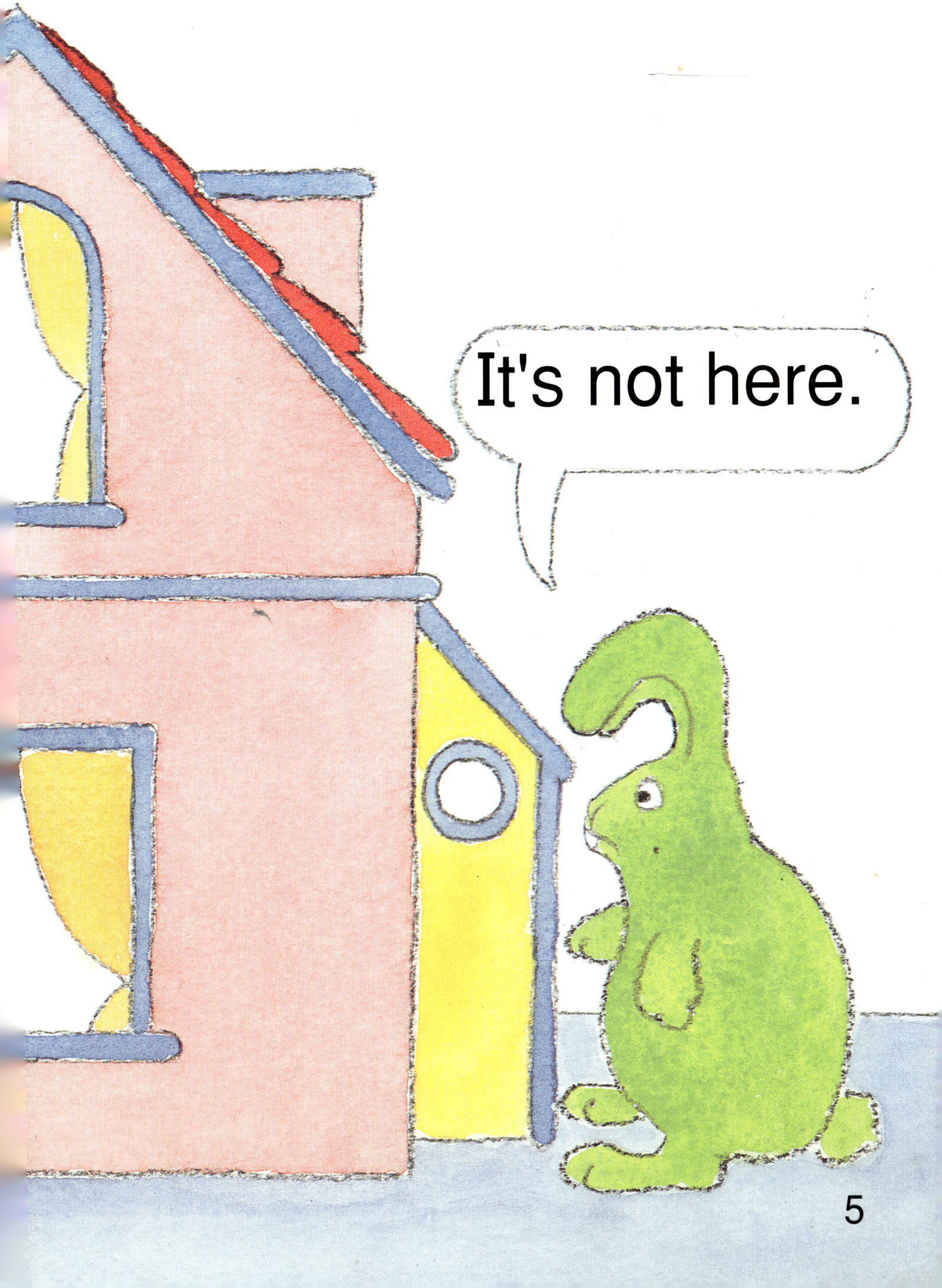
It's not here.

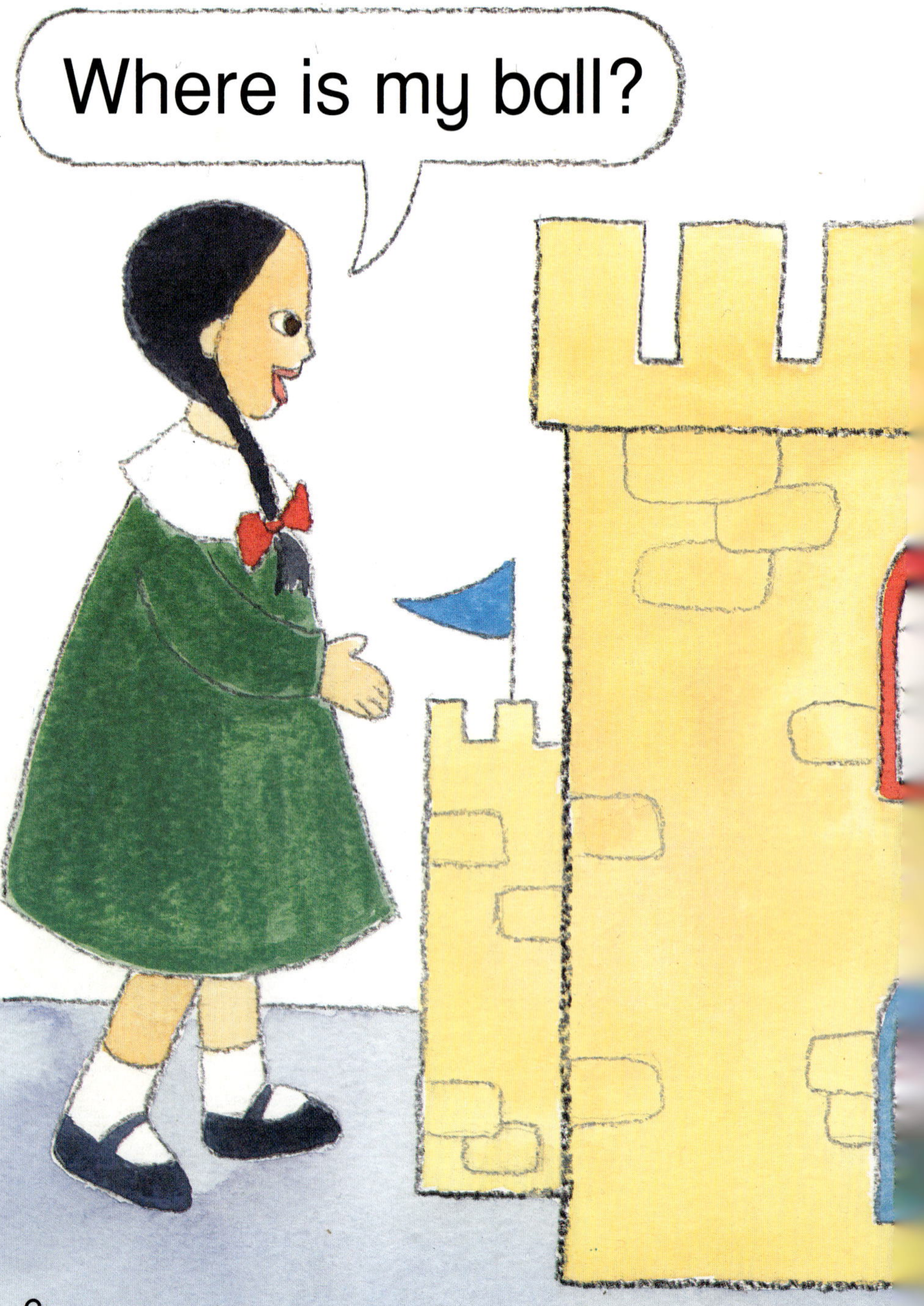
Where is my ball?

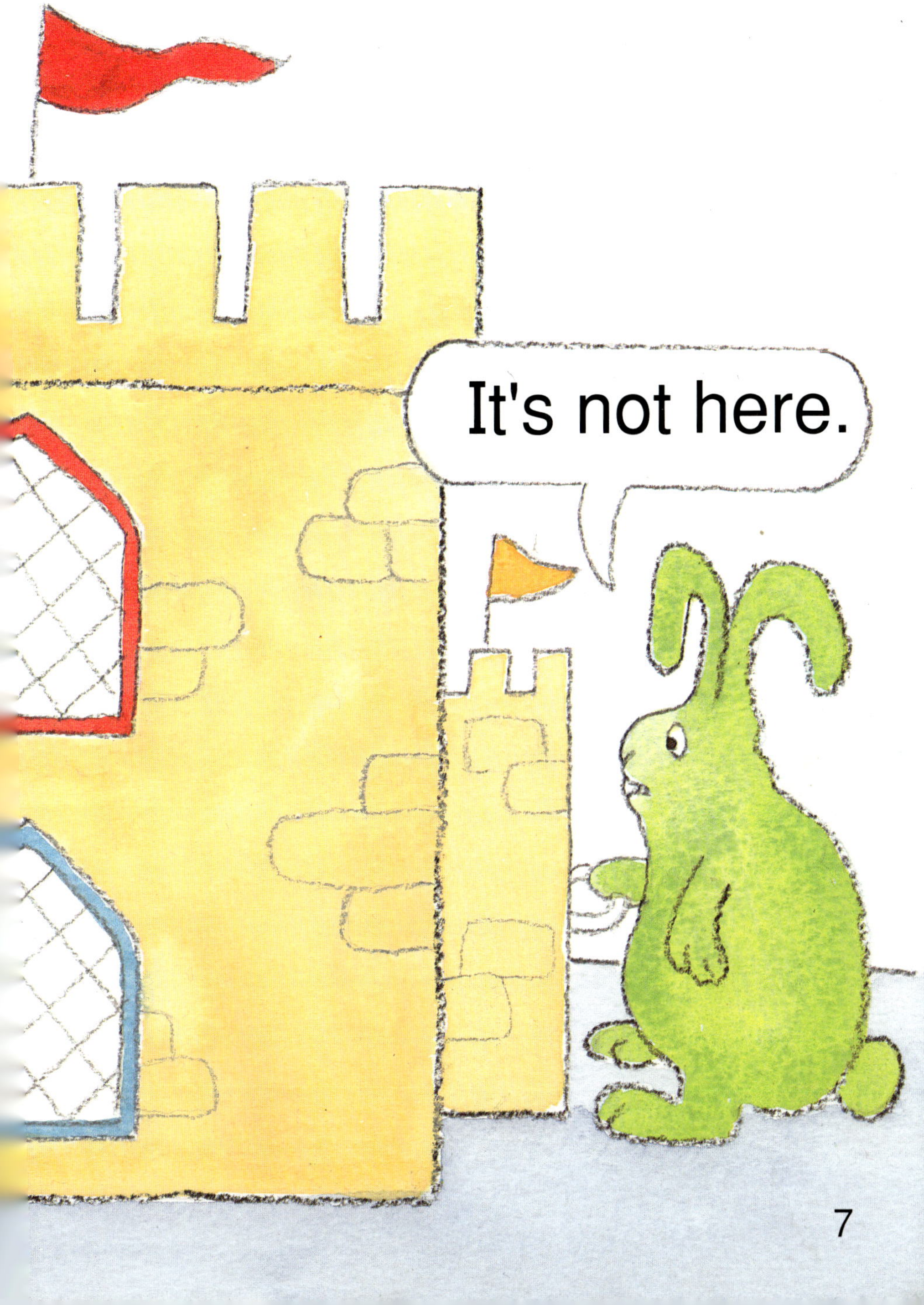
It's not here.

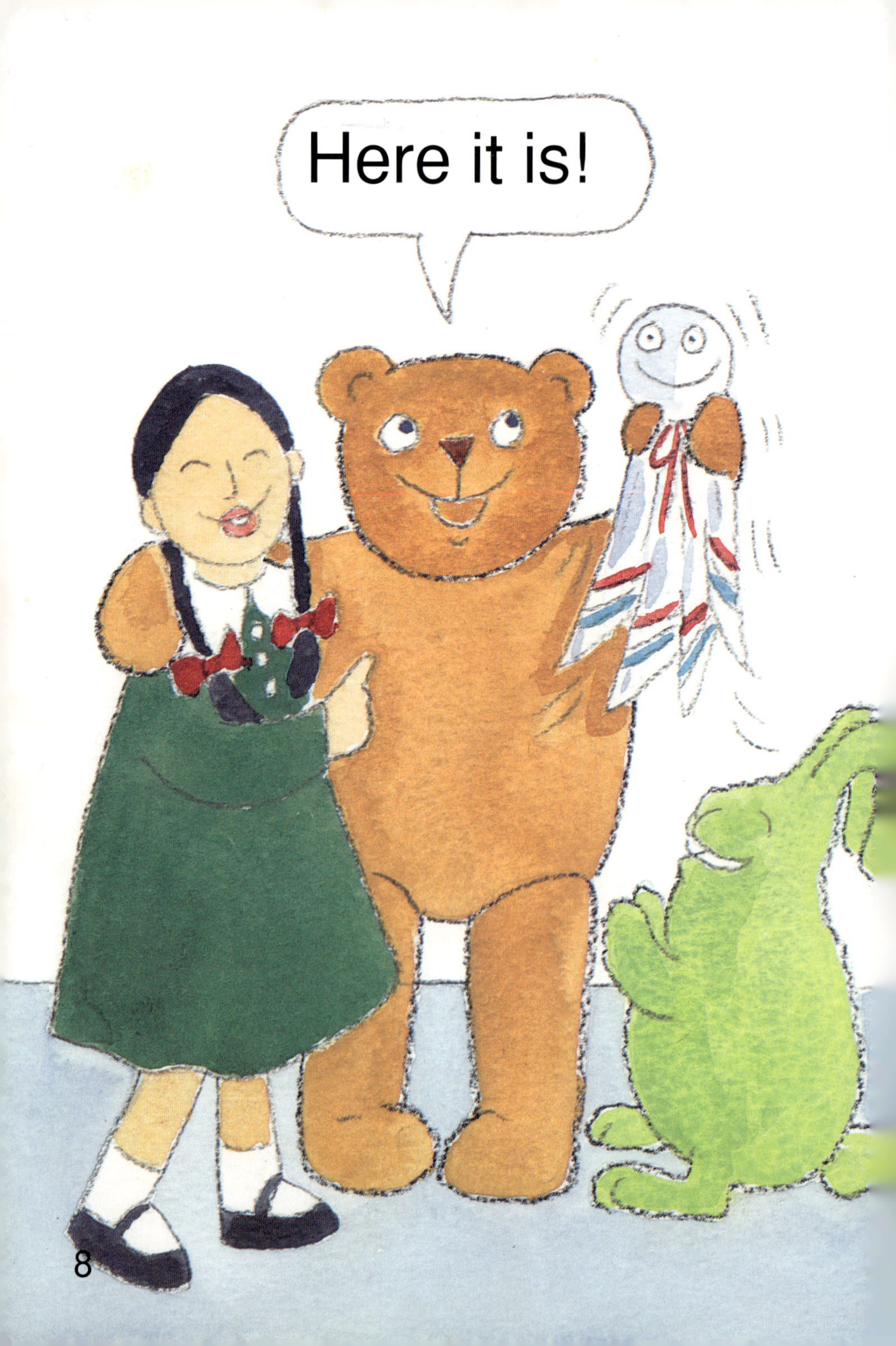
Here it is!